DISCOVER 🐾 DOGS WITH THE AMERICAN CANINE ASSOCIATION

I LIKE
IRISH WOLFHOUNDS!

Linda Bozzo

Published in 2018 by Enslow Publishing, LLC.
101 W. 23rd Street, Suite 240, New York, NY 10011

Library of Congress Cataloging-in-Publication Data

Names: Bozzo, Linda, author.
Title: I like Irish wolfhounds! / Linda Bozzo.
Description: New York : Enslow Publishing, 2018. | Series: Discover dogs with the American Canine Association | Includes bibliographical references and index. | Audience: Grades K to 3.
Identifiers: LCCN 2017001306 | ISBN 9780766086425 (library-bound) | ISBN 9780766088771 (pbk.) | ISBN 9780766088719 (6-pack)
Subjects: LCSH: Irish wolfhound—Juvenile literature.
Classification: LCC SF429.I85 B69 2017 | DDC 636.753/5—dc23
LC record available at https://lccn.loc.gov/2017001306

Printed in the United States of America

To Our Readers: We have done our best to make sure all websites in this book were active and appropriate when we went to press. However, the author and the publisher have no control over and assume no liability for the material available on those websites or on any websites they may link to. Any comments or suggestions can be sent by email to customerservice@enslow.com.

Enslow Publishing
101 W. 23rd Street
Suite 240
New York, NY 10011
USA

enslow.com

CONTENTS

IS AN IRISH WOLFHOUND RIGHT FOR YOU?

Irish wolfhounds are friendly and gentle dogs. They are good with children. If you have a large living space, an Irish wolfhound may be right for you!

Irish wolfhounds are probably the tallest of all dog breeds. Make sure your family owns a car large enough to carry your Irish wolfhound.

A DOG OR A PUPPY?

Careful training for puppies is important. If you do not have time to train a puppy, an older Irish wolfhound may be better for your family.

Irish wolfhound puppies grow very large very quickly. This takes a lot of energy, so these puppies sleep a lot.

LOVING YOUR IRISH WOLFHOUND

Love your Irish wolfhound by taking a walk or sharing a couch with him.

The Irish wolfhound is known as the "gentle giant."

EXERCISE

Irish wolfhounds are quiet dogs that like to be indoors. But they will also enjoy a run in the yard or walks on a **leash**. Games, like **fetch**, are fun for both you and your dog.

Adult Irish wolfhounds need very little playtime.

FEEDING YOUR IRISH WOLFHOUND

Irish wolfhounds can be fed wet or dry dog food. Ask a **veterinarian** (vet), a doctor for animals, which food is best for your dog and how much to feed her. Larger breeds can have stomach problems from eating too much during one meal.

Give your Irish wolfhound fresh, clean water every day.

Remember to keep your dog's food and water dishes clean. Dirty dishes can make a dog sick.

Do not feed your dog people food. It can make her sick.

Your new dog will need:

a collar with a tag

a bed

a brush

food and water dishes

a leash

toys

GROOMING

Irish wolfhounds **shed** very little. This means their hair doesn't fall out much. Irish wolfhounds need to be brushed to keep them clean and looking their best.

Your dog will need a bath every so often. Use a gentle soap made just for dogs. An Irish wolfhound's nails need to be clipped. A vet or **groomer** can show you how. Your dog's ears should be cleaned and her teeth should be brushed by an adult.

WHAT YOU SHOULD KNOW

Irish wolfhounds need a soft place to lie on.

Irish wolfhounds like being with other dogs. They are good with other pets.

Giant breeds, such as the Irish wolfhound, don't live as long as other breeds. They live around six to eight years.

Because of their size, Irish wolfhounds are not for everyone!

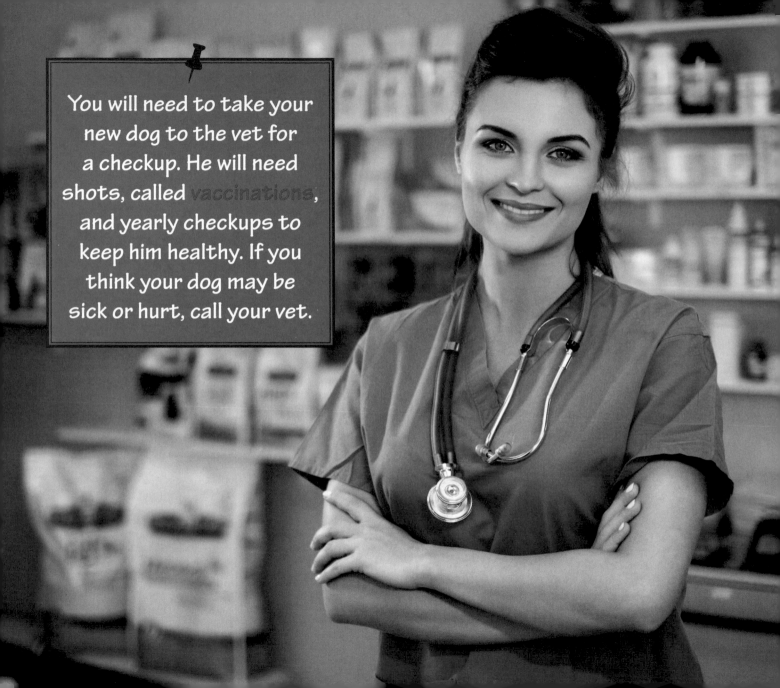

You will need to take your new dog to the vet for a checkup. He will need shots, called vaccinations, and yearly checkups to keep him healthy. If you think your dog may be sick or hurt, call your vet.

A GOOD FRIEND

If you take good care of your Irish wolfhound, you will have a loving friend for years.

NOTE TO PARENTS

It is important to consider having your dog spayed or neutered when the dog is young. Spaying and neutering are operations that prevent unwanted puppies and can help improve the overall health of your dog.

It is also a good idea to microchip your dog, in case he or she gets lost. A vet will implant a microchip under the skin containing an identification number that can be scanned at a vet's office or animal shelter. The microchip registry is contacted and the company uses the ID number to look up your information from a database.

Some towns require licenses for dogs, so be sure to check with your town clerk.

For more information, speak with a vet.

There are many dogs, young and old, waiting to be adopted from animal shelters and rescue groups.

fetch To go after a toy and bring it back.

groomer A person who bathes and brushes dogs.

leash A chain or strap that attaches to the dog's collar.

shed When dog hair falls out so new hair can grow.

vaccinations Shots that dogs need to stay healthy.

veterinarian (vet) A doctor for animals.

Read About Dogs

Books

Morey, Allan, and Emily Crain. *Irish Wolfhounds*. North Mankato, MN: Capstone Press, 2016.

Nelson, Kristen Rajczak. *Irish Wolfhounds*. New York, NY: Gareth Stevens, 2012.

Websites

American Canine Association Inc., Kids Corner
www.acakids.com
Visit the official website of the American Canine Association.

National Geographic for Kids, Pet Central
kids.nationalgeographic.com / explore / pet-central /
Learn more about dogs and other pets at the official site of the National Geographic Society for Kids.

INDEX